WILD DOGS

AN IMAGINATION LIBRARY SERIES

by Victor Gentle and Janet Perry

Gareth Stevens Publishing
A WORLD ALMANAC EDUCATION GROUP COMPANY

Please visit our web site at: www.garethstevens.com
For a free color catalog describing Gareth Stevens Publishing's
list of high-quality books and multimedia programs,
call 1-800-542-2595 or fax your request to (414) 332-3567.

Library of Congress Cataloging-in-Publication Data

Gentle, Victor.
    Jackals / by Victor Gentle and Janet Perry.
       p. cm. — (Wild dogs: an imagination library series)
    Includes bibliographical references and index.
    Summary: An introduction to the physical characteristics and behavior of jackals.
    ISBN 0-8368-3097-0 (lib. bdg.)
    1. Jackals—Juvenile literature. [1. Jackals.] I. Perry, Janet. II. Title.
QL737.C22G4468   2002
599.77'2—dc21
                                                    2001054952

First published in 2002 by
Gareth Stevens Publishing
A World Almanac Education Group Company
330 West Olive Street, Suite 100
Milwaukee, WI 53212 USA

Text: Victor Gentle and Janet Perry
Page layout: Victor Gentle, Janet Perry, and Tammy Gruenewald
Cover design: Tammy Gruenewald
Series editor: Catherine Gardner
Picture Researcher: Diane Laska-Swanke

Photo credits: Cover (main) © Joe McDonald; cover (background) Diane Laska-Swanke; pp. 5
(main, bottom inset), 9, 13, 17 © Joe McDonald/Visuals Unlimited; p. 5 (top inset) © Lockwood &
Dattatri/BBC Natural History Unit; p. 7 © Tony Heald/BBC Natural History Unit; p. 11 © Susan
Stockwell/RSPCA Photolibrary; p. 15 © Karl Amman/BBC Natural History Unit; p. 19 © Don
Davies/RSPCA Photolibrary; p. 21 © Charles McRae/Visuals Unlimited

Printed in the United States of America

1 2 3 4 5 6 7 8 9 06 05 04 03 02

Front cover: Now *that* looks interesting! What
do you think has grabbed the attention of this
handsome pair of black-backed jackal pups?

TABLE OF CONTENTS

Words that appear in the glossary are printed in **boldface** type the first time they occur in the text.

FAR AND WIDE, WET AND DRY

Some jackals live in the Middle East and southern Asia, but most **species** of jackals live in Africa. Each species prefers a different **habitat**, and some are quite choosy about the place they call home.

Black-backed jackals live only in Africa and like dry areas, even deserts. Side-striped jackals also live only in Africa, but they prefer moist woods and the moister parts of grasslands. Golden jackals live in the Middle East, Asia, and Africa — anywhere they can find open country with trees, brush, and grass. There is also a wild dog sometimes called a Simien jackal. It is not really a jackal, though. It is a kind of wolf.

What's in a name? Is the golden jackal's coat really golden? Is the black-backed jackal's back all black? What color is the side-striped jackal's stripe?

A TASTE FOR ALMOST ANYTHING

What jackals eat depends a lot on where they live. Jackals eat food they can find easily. Mostly, jackals catch many small animals, including **gazelle** calves, hares, mice, birds, frogs, and insects. They also eat eggs, fruits, and seeds.

Jackals are famous **scavengers**. They will eat meat from animals they did not kill. Often, these animals are large **prey**, like zebras or wildebeests, that are killed by other **predators**.

A black-backed jackal warns a vulture to stay back. Both are scavengers, fighting for an easy meal. The zebra was killed by another predator.

TWO JACKALS ARE BETTER THAN ONE

When a jackal hunts for food, it usually goes alone and chooses small prey. To hunt larger prey, like a gazelle calf, it pays to team up. Two jackals hunting together catch their prey much more often than a jackal hunting by itself.

Some kinds of wild dogs, like wolves, choose big prey and live in large groups, called packs. On the other hand, jackals hunt smaller prey and live alone, in pairs, or in small family groups.

A black-backed jackal feeds on a gazelle calf in the Masai Mara Game Reserve in eastern Africa. Jackals usually cannot catch adult gazelles.

JACKAL JIVE

To **communicate** with their families, jackals yelp, howl, bark, and scream. They can be a noisy bunch. Each species uses different sounds to send the same kinds of messages. Their sounds help them warn of danger, share food, or just keep in touch.

Black-backed jackals yelp to tell others where they are. Golden jackals howl. Side-striped jackals are quieter than their golden or black-backed cousins. They never howl. They just bark a few times to send a message.

Like all dogs, jackals also use their bodies to communicate with one another. The jackal on the right is signaling, "OK, OK, you're the boss."

SPOUSES AND SPACES

Jackals also communicate with smells, or scents. They mark their **territory** to tell other jackals to stay away. Their territory is about 1 to 2 square miles (2.5 to 5 square kilometers).

When a young male and female jackal meet, they choose and mark a territory together. Jackals mostly pair up for life. They **mate** once a year.

While the female is **pregnant**, the jackals look for a **den**. They choose a sheltered spot, dig a hole, or take over a burrow dug by another animal.

This happy pair of jackals lives in southwest Africa, in a national park where tourists' garbage cans give them more chances to find food.

JACKAL JUNIORS

Usually, a jackal has four to six pups in a **litter**. A golden jackal may have up to nine. The pups drink their mother's milk from the day they are born.

Two-week-old pups come out from the den and are ready to try solid food. To feed young pups, adults eat after a hunt, return to the den, and **regurgitate** the food. Ten-week-old jackals stop **nursing**. When they are twelve weeks old, pups go on "field trips" to hunt with their parents.

This black-backed jackal mom gives her baby's face a good wash. You can see from the mother's coat why these jackals are also called "silver-backed."

JACKAL HELPERS

After ten or eleven months, many young jackals leave home. Some young jackals, however, stay with their parents, who soon have a new litter of pups. The young jackals become "helpers" who feed and protect the new pups.

While the mother and father search for food, the helpers stay with the pups. Helpers watch for danger and warn pups to hide. Helpers also chase away **hyenas** and other predators that snatch unprotected pups. Pups with helpers are much more likely to survive than pups born in families without helpers.

Black-backed jackal pups hang out at their den in the Masai Mara Game Reserve. Soon, these pups will be ready to hunt with the adults.

JACKAL HAZARDS

Jackals face many hazards. Leopards, hyenas, and eagles are among their worst natural enemies. Disease can wipe out many jackals in an area, all at once. Drought kills, too.

Jackal pups face even more dangers. Sometimes, other jackals kill them. Heavy rains flood dens and drown them.

Humans are the biggest threat of all. Some people hunt jackals for furs. Farmers kill jackals because jackals sometimes kill farm animals. People take over land that jackals need for hunting.

A hyena chases a black-backed jackal from food. Hyenas can kill a lone jackal, so it's a good idea for jackals to keep their distance from hyenas.

JACKALS AND PEOPLE

There are many threats to jackals, but the number of jackals has held steady in recent years. Still, they will not survive if people keep killing jackals instead of understanding them.

Getting rid of jackals can cause problems. In Israel, some people killed lots of jackals to protect their farm animals. But jackals eat snakes. When the jackals were gone, more people got snakebites.

People need to understand more about the ways animals are connected. People must find more ways to share the planet with animals.

A jackal stands by a water hole in Etosha National Park in Namibia. Here, it is alert to its natural foes and safe from humans.

MORE TO READ AND VIEW

Books (Nonfiction) *The Family Howl.* Betty Dineen (Macmillan)
Jackal Woman: Exploring the World of Jackals.
   Laurence P. Pringle (Atheneum)
Wild Dogs. Timothy L. Biel (Creative Education)
Wild Dogs (series). Victor Gentle and Janet Perry
   (Gareth Stevens)
Your Dog's Wild Cousins. Hope Ryden (Penguin Putnam)

Books (Fiction) *The Blue Jackal.* Mehlli Gobhai (Prentice-Hall)
Jackal Wants Everything. Sweet Pickles (series). Jacquelyn Reinach
   (Holt, Rinehart & Winston)

Books (Activity) *Dogs of the Wild* (coloring book). Peter M. Spizzirri (Spizzirri)

Videos (Nonfiction) *Etosha, Africa's Untamed Wilderness. Living Edens* (series).
   (PBS Home Video)
Wings over the Serengeti. (National Geographic)

PLACES TO VISIT, WRITE, OR CALL

You can learn lots about jackals at zoos and museums. Call or write to the zoos to find out about their jackals and their plans to preserve jackals in the wild. Better yet, go visit them yourself! The Field Museum has great exhibits on many African predators and prey.

Kansas City Zoo
Swope Park, 6800 Zoo Drive
Kansas City, MO 64132-4200
(816) 513-5700

Oklahoma City Zoological Park
2101 E. 50th Street
Oklahoma City, OK 73111-7106
(405) 424-3344

The Field Museum
1400 S. Lake Shore Drive
Chicago, IL 60605-2496
(312) 922-9410

WEB SITES

If you have your own computer and Internet access, great! If not, most libraries have Internet access. The Internet changes every day, and web sites come and go. We believe the following sites are likely to last and give the best, most appropriate links for readers to find out more about jackals and other wild dogs around the world.

To get started finding web sites about jackals, choose a general search engine. You can plug words into the search engine and see what it finds for you. Some words related to jackals are: *jackals, savannas,* and *African wildlife.*

www.yahooligans.com

This is a huge search engine and a great research tool for anything you might want to know. For information on jackals, click on <u>Animals</u> under the <u>Science & Nature</u> heading. From the Animals page, you can see or hear jackals and other wild dogs by clicking on <u>Animal Sounds</u> or <u>Animal Pictures</u>.

dmoz.org/Recreation/Pets/Dogs/Wild_Dogs

"*dmoz.org*" gives lists of web sites chosen by people rather than a search engine. This is a page listing web sites where you can find lots of information about wild dogs. Click on *jackals* as well as some of the *canid* sites listed. Most have pictures or diagrams, and some are just for kids. See which ones work for you.

www.awf.org/wildlives

This is the African Wildlife Foundation page. Learn about many different wild African animals here, including jackals.

www.hunting-safari.co.za/sounds_of_africa.htm

This site has some great African animal sounds including the sound of the black-backed jackal.

www.pbs.org/wnet/nature/jackals

Jackals of the African Crater is a PBS web site that features information on the lives of jackals and on the Jackal Woman, a scientist who studies jackals.

GLOSSARY

You can find these words on the pages listed. Reading a word in a sentence helps you understand it even better.

communicate (kuh-MYOO-nuh-KAYT) — share information 10, 12

den (DEN) — place where animals give birth, hide their young, and sleep 12, 14, 16, 18

gazelle (guh-ZEL) — quick, graceful antelope with long, twisted horns 6, 8

habitat (HAB-uh-tat) — place that has the things an animal needs to live 4

hyenas (hye-EE-nuhs) — animals that howl, scavenge, and look like big dogs 16, 18

litter (LIT-ur) — group of pups born at the same time to the same mother 14, 16

mate (MAYT) — come together to make babies 12

nursing (NURS-ing) — feeding milk to pups 14

predators (PRED-uh-turs) — animals that hunt other animals for food 6, 16

pregnant (PREG-nuhnt) — having babies growing inside the mother animal 12

prey (PRAY) — animals that are hunted by other animals for food 6, 8

regurgitate (ree-GUR-juh-tayt) — to bring up swallowed food for a pup to eat 14

scavengers (SKAV-uhn-jurs) — animals that eat the remains of animals that were killed by another animal or died naturally 6

species (SPEE-shees) — a group of plants or animals that are alike in many ways 4, 10

territory (TER-uh-tor-ee) — area of land that an animal (or group of animals) marks out as its hunting ground 12

INDEX